(

G000277492

llow of
iter. In
nd was
r. Her
eceived
blished
s, tele-
claimed
Pushkin
Russias
)1) was
einstein
s across
iouncil,
Rocke-
ve been
)2) was
vel *The*
1 2010.
iendent
)95 was

Please return on or before the latest date above.
You can renew online at www.kent.gov.uk/libs
or by phone 08458 247 200

STOMER SERVICE EXCELLENCE   **Libraries & Archives**

Also by Elaine Feinstein from Carcanet Press

Daylight
Gold
Selected Poems
Collected Poems and Translations
Talking to the Dead
The Russian Jerusalem

As translator
Bride of Ice: Selected Poems of Marina Tsvetaeva

As editor
After Pushkin

ELAINE FEINSTEIN

Cities

CARCANET

Acknowledgements

Some of these poems have appeared in *The Guardian, Jewish Quarterly, The Liberal, Notre Dame Review, PN Review, Poetry London, Poetry Review, Saudade: An Anthology of Fado Poetry, The Spectator, The Times Literary Supplement* and *Wasifiri*.

The author thanks Judith Willson for the care she has taken throughout the production

First published in Great Britain in 2010 by
Carcanet Press Limited
Alliance House
Cross Street
Manchester M2 7AQ

A CIP catalogue record for this book is available from the British Library
ISBN 978 1 84777 061 5

The publisher acknowledges financial assistance from Arts Council England

Supported by
**ARTS COUNCIL
ENGLAND**

Typeset by XL Publishing Services, Tiverton
Printed and bound in England by SRP Ltd, Exeter

for Michael

Contents

Migrations

1

In late March, birds from the Gambia,
white throat warblers, who wintered in
the branches of a feathery acacia;
Mandelstam's goldfinch; pink foot
geese from the Arctic. All
arrive using the stars, along
flyways old as Homer and Jeremiah.

2

Avian immigration is down this year,
but humans still have reasons to move on,
the usual chronicle of poverty, enemies,
or ominous skies the colour of tobacco.
They arrive in London with battered luggage,
and eyes dark as black cherries

holding fast to old religions
and histories, remembering
the shock of being hunted in the streets,
the pain at leaving their dead
in broken cemeteries, their resilience
hardwired as birds' skill in navigation.

On the Jubilee line, a black woman
has the profile of a wood carving from Benin.
In Willesden Green, *Polski delikatesy*, or a grocer
piling up African vegetables. An English woman
buys hot ginger and white radish: the filigree
of migration, symbiosis, assimilation.

3

All my grandparents came from Odessa
a century ago, spoke little English,
and were doubtless suspect as foreigners
– probably anarchist or Bolshevik –
very likely to be dreaming of bombs.
It is never easy to be a stranger,

to be split between loneliness
and disloyalty, to be impatient
with dogma, yet still distrusted
in a world which prefers to be secular.
When I listen to the gaiety of Klezmer,
I understand why migrants like ghettos.

These people come from desperate countries
where flies walk over the faces of sick children,
and even here in Britain the luckless
will find gangmasters to arrange
work in mudflats as cockle pickers.
Why should they care my ancestors

had a long history of crossing borders,
when I am settled now after all those journeys?
And why do I want to make common cause
with them anyway? Only because I remember
how easily the civil world turns brutal.
If it does, we shall have the same enemies.

Wartime Leicester

1

Who is that child from a leafy Stoneygate garden,
leaving the sunken lawns and alpine rockery
to explore a patch of wild ground over the fence?

She crawls on the ground like an Indian tracker,
with powdery earth hurting her wide eyes,
or finds a delicate way up the pear tree branches,

her face absorbed. I remember the story she moves in:
the dream of a perilous world
in which she can only live with the skills of a boy.

Her father is unhappy, because she takes no pleasure
in the garden he laid out with such euphoria,
his magnificent fruit trees: Victoria plum and Coxes.

His only daughter stubbornly prefers
to steal redcurrants from the wild brambles
which prickle her tongue and may well poison her.

2

When war comes, streetlights go out at night.
Even the Clock Tower is dark –
the electric sparks from a tram are blue as starlight.

In school, when a bell sounds for air raid practice,
the girls file over the hockey pitch
into concrete bunkers carrying satchels of goodies:

Sunpat raisins, fruity chocolate blobs.
In the heady smell of earth,
they gossip avidly. She is growing up.

At fourteen, she colours her lips dark red.
and hoists her small breasts
for the Palais de Danse, where she learns

the language of market boys from the East End,
and how to imitate
loose limbed Americans who move like dancers.

Her chrysalis conceals the girl I am
as I begin to read at nights:
Hamlet, John Keats, Omar Khayyam.

Cambridge, 1949

Look, how she teeters in a tight skirt
on high heels over the cobbled street,
past Heffers' gabled windows and knobbly glass,
the music of wartime dance bands still inside her –
what does she know of madrigals and choirs,
my adolescent self, in her first term?
She dreams of Soho clubs and Raymond Chandler.

Dismissing girls in tweedy clothes as dowdy,
she does not recognise the family names
connected into webs of social power; altogether
too unworldly to be a Marrano,
she says grace at High Table as a Scholar,
giggling, over wet lettuce and beetroot,
unaware of any reserve around her.

Yet as she reads in her Newnham room the metaphysical
poets claim her, and she enters
the Christian centuries with Donne and Herbert,
filled with an unexpected terror.
What if it were all true ? The angels
on the shore, the judgement,
the dismissal and her secular world denied?

What if this present were the world's last night?
The paradise of leaf dust and wood smoke
would vanish in the darker truth behind.
Unprotected by her own rituals
or any reading in the Sciences, she is caught
in a history told by eloquent strangers:
she prays alongside Gerard Manley Hopkins,

until a Fulbright student from New York
rescues her with mockery, and
lends her Pound's miraculous *Cathay*
which staggers her with the sad,
erotic beauty of an ancient culture
while he with skilful fingers,
teaches her in the shade of willow trees
how to explore further outside the syllabus.

Portugal Place, Cambridge

Everything began in that fairytale house
of tilted rooms with a single strand
of a golden helix hanging by the entrance.

Everything: babies, friendship, fun,
a naked woman scrawled on the bath,
– an indelible, eye-popping invitation –

the raffish parties of the Obscene Potter,
John Gayer Anderson, in Waterbeach,
where Nobel scientists enjoyed au pair girls.

Our kitchen, floored with stone, below
street level, was never empty
and the music of Georges Brassens, offering

his sweet almond tree to the whole *quartier*
filled us with France – as for me
there it was: the first salt lick of poetry.

Piaf in Babraham

The pin is loose that holds the climbing rose.
It crackles on the glass. I stare outside
at a single wet goat with oblong eyes:
bemused – a young wife and mother,
beyond the Gogs – and my own story over.

The bole and branches of the trees are smooth
– like water pipes – in sodium light.
The pop and bubble of children's
television rises up the stairs.
I scribble, while a voice reaches into me,

Edith Piaf, and the songs she chose, of failed
loves, loneliness, poverty.
I long for her Paris streets, and the glamour
of a woman who never had safety
to lose – the thin child with a monstrous voice

rattling centimes in a hat – those walls of mirrors
in grand restaurants – the Dietrich eyebrows
– even the drug pallor. All of it was her choice,
a tiny woman in a black dress,
with an audience ready to watch her collapse on stage.

Rien, je ne regrette rien. While I, in bland
everyday disorder, listen
to the soaring triumph in her voice, knowing
she has only earned that elation, because
she learned to sell her ordinary life for applause.

At the Chelsea

A first sleepless glimpse of New York:
shiny dawn streets, pink towers,
like creatures from another planet,
the movement of cars beating
like a pulse between traffic lights.

The Chelsea charges writers a low rent since
Dylan Thomas died there in his dreams.
The walls are three foot thick, we are assured,
so you won't be disturbed
by loud music. Or screams.

Jazz on 42nd Street with Charlie Mingus,
Betty Carter singing in the Village,
Nicholas Ray, mistakenly hoping we might
be film magnates, retreating to
the bedroom, to bind his arm with a tourniquet.

Virgil Thomson had a flat on the top floor.
He took us to watch a play
called *Screw* at the Lincoln Center. There,
two actors read from a tool manual –
the only disappointment in our whole visit –
and even then, at least unusual.

Basel

Did I like the Swiss? In the cinema,
they were the good guys, you were safe,
if only you could ski across their border.
That summer, our train pulled over the Rhine
– waters brown after rain –
into a city with toy trams and shop glitter

to be astonished by European plenty:
glum England suddenly forgotten.
La Roche on Grenzacherstrasse was the patron
– not the floodlit Münster where Erasmus lies,
under tiles of green and golden leaves –
pharmacy funding labs of pure science.

Poles and Czechs in Molecular Biology,
made fun of Baseler proprieties –
those civic fingers shaken at pedestrians –
and we grew as wild as the hippies
on Barfüsserplatz. Some nights
dining in the Rheinkeller, looking up the hillside

to the Münster on its darkness of rich foliage
we remembered the old dangers
but we spoke of Paracelsus and his travels
not bribes at wartime borders nor the Reformer
zeal of clever Swiss bankers. For six months
we lived under the sun of Ecclesiastes!

Jerusalem

1

Your stones hold the glow of a June sun
until the desert night drops
a dark blue cloak over the streets

abruptly, as always in the Levant.
When I saw you first,
barbed wire threaded your heart,

and the clarity of your stars pierced me –
like an ancient tribal God.
I sold back all my silver trinkets

so I could wander the narrow alleys
with your white dust
in my sandals for a few days longer,

drink mint tea with my Moroccan lover
under Jordanian guns before
I left for rainy London and the man I married.

2 Abu Tor

We flew together, after the Six Day War,
– with an unfamiliar salt on our lips –
to visit Arieh Sachs, in Abu Tor
above the stone strewn valley of Cedron,
whose waters lead to the Valley of Hinnom,

supposedly the scene of the Last Judgement.
Arieh was holding a drinks party
fired by the peculiar astonishment,
of a boy who has taken on the school bully,
and floored him with an unexpected blow.

We argued until it was dawn with poet
conscripts: about courage and ghettos,
Warsaw and Sobibor. We talked
of peace, the loss of close friends
and the dangerous energy men find in war.

Nobody spoke of Victory with elation,
or pretended local hatreds had gone away.
At first light, we set off along Nablus road
for the American Colony hotel
a Pasha's palace, where the journalists stay.

In Mishkenot Sha'ananim twenty years on
at the time of the first *intifada*
Amichai advised us sensibly:

Yes, go into the Old City
but not too often, and not
for long. When the shutters

begin to come down, remember
the shopkeepers are also afraid of gunmen.
So don't barter after you hear the bell.

In Mahane Yehuda, a few old Russian men
are playing *shesh besh* in the courtyard.

I am alone, here for a festival,
shivering in a light coat.

April is often cold in Jerusalem
But that's not why.
I met my old boyfriend *relevant to nee* }
which was disappointing.

But that's not it. This time I saw Jerusalem
was no longer a secular city,

but part of the fanatic Middle East.
And I was frightened. Would the Lord protect her?

form of rain fall?

5 Postscript, London

Rain in August, and the rolling news
    shows rubble in Lebanon,
        and journalists fired up

by a war which plays better than the World Cup
    for adrenalin, raw excitement
        and indignation,

against Israel mainly, which is safely at a distance –
    like Czechoslovakia in the thirties –
        while London is confused on its fault line,

afraid tectonic plates may shift again, and
    bring another day, as red as hatred
        and white as death.

A flick of silver high in clear sky.
    We look up and imagine:
        Blood. Bone. Brain. Breath.

Warsaw, 1973

Wajda's city of ashes and diamonds, where
a fairground wheel once turned
to carnival music while the ghetto burned.

Now postilions in snuff coloured livery.
wait for tourists, few in '73.
In the Writers' House someone has invented

a lost empire of courtesy, with cartoons
on green baize walls, though
a chandelier has crystals cloudy as salt.

A piano is playing Chopin. His courage
and death sound in the narrow streets,
where our cousin, Hannah Krall, survived the war,

hidden by clients of her mother's beauty salon.
Fifty families, she tells us solemnly,
and it was always the men who insisted I move on.

Lublin, 1973

for Arnold

When Czesław Miłosz read in London
you told him his voice was like
your grandmother's. His smile resembled yours.
You were never scared of genius
and he was gentle with you, explaining:

The Polish accent sticks to the palate
across three languages.

In Lublin, your ancestral city, we found
the family name not yet forgotten,
though the yellow house on the town square
was long since broken up into flats,
heated by a central blue tiled stove.

Zimmerman? the tenants say.
Yes, we remember them.

A short drive to Majdanek, in the outskirts.
Your cousin had given us
the exact location of the gas chamber
so we could stand in the same place
and know what they were feeling.

Are those fingernail marks
on the cement ceiling?

Krakow, 1973

Fair Rynek, yellow stone and floodlit arches!
The metal trumpeter still plays on the hour,
as if an arrow had not found his throat,

or the Germans entered the city. In
Kazimierz there are no ghosts
– they have moved to Oswiecim –

and while the Russians hold Krakow
fast in their hegemony
no one restores shop fronts of Jewish bistros.

The bricks show under plaster. This was
Schindler's playground once;
but his factories on Lipowska stand empty.

And there is no nostalgia. Our minders show us
the theatre of Andrzej Wajda
that night staging Kafka's *Trial*

against white sheets and sudden darkness –
at the climax there is a splash of red.
Soberly, we drink vodka with the actors.

Budapest

1

Before the Soviet grip began to slacken
– most conquerors go, eventually, even the Turks,
who whitewashed the frescoes in Matthias Church,
leaving columns of Moorish terracotta –
I stayed at the Gellert, a spa hotel, with a green

nymph poised in the marble lobby. Beneath the floor
hot springs, blue pools smelling of sulphur;
and an expressionless country girl waiting stolidly
to pummel hotel guests in muddy water.
This city always beckoned stories from me;

I watched the porno cabaret beneath the Astoria,
or sat in Gerbeau's café in Vörösmarty.
Girls with shoes and handbags of matching leather
sauntered past in a flirtatious party.
And I invented a history I might have shared,

a pink-lit past of velvet drapes, and corded
bell pushes, where in my fantasy
assimilated relatives took pleasure
in an enchanted, unfamiliar
world where a bold wit counted more than ancestry.

Was it ever so? This Habsburg city. whose coffee
and pastries once equalled Vienna,
still preserved, even in Soviet Hungary
an air of permissive, shabby splendour –
but nowhere in Central Europe was truly tolerant,

as Marrano ghosts rise to remind me: their disguise
was permeable, the Arrow Cross
assiduous; of the prominent, most were taken,
and – like those rich Hungarian soups seasoned
with paprika and too much pork fat – that knowledge sickens.

2

In the messy flat of Janos Pilinszky,
his most loved records lie
without sleeves, horizontal
on his bookshelves. See,

his parchment face is bloodless,
lit like a lamp from within,
his bones fine, his lips
shrewdly curved, humorous.

In his poetry, men are harnessed
to a cart, or watch an execution.
A tin cup tips over in the straw.
He lives in the guilt of witness,

still wanting to write
but as if he remained silent.
His companions at night:
Alyosha – or Stavrogin.

He longs for the Lord,
to bury him in his embrace
but *the old are alone*, he says,
and believe in nothing.

3

We follow tramlines up to the Castle district,
walking with a Cambridge friend whose
family name is part of Hungarian history.

Trees. Birds. Leaf smells. Then the Danube
with all its bridges shining there below us.
In the open air, it is safe enough to discuss

Lukács and the fierce Marxist reasoning
which led him sadly to reject Franz Kafka.
If anyone approaches us too closely,

he points out holes in the walls of the Hilton.
Hungarians do not disguise the war
and in Buda leave the scars of shelling visible.

Uphill, he shows us the turn of the rails where
his grandfather was shot as a member
of the Magyar Parliament early in the century.

And this is his family home, though
he only has a flat in part of it. Within,
a Pitt Rivers pile of ancestral goodies:

carved jade, a horn of Chinese ivory, shelves
of hand-painted country jugs loved by his mother.
He smiles, like a handsome, spoiled, child

confessing he is homesick for the West
and has some problems at his Institute,
We drink plum brandy. His wife

had stuffed mushrooms, and wrapped
cream cheese in spinach for us. I can't
remember her face, only that she is sad.

Z., our host, is afraid we'll come to harm.
He takes us by car to the conference dinner
where Gypsies come to the table with violins,
their fingers flickering through Mozart and Brahms

– or Yiddish tunes if they recognise Americans.
Z. doesn't like the Roma. He complains
There are too many and they live in squalor.
His own house, which is bare and steam-cleaned,

he and his wife work twelve hours a day to pay for.
His eyes are hot and blue. He confesses how much
he dislikes the sloppiness of Budapest. For himself,
he is proud to be born in Debreczen

where people plan their lives like good peasants.
He offers to drive us there across the *puszta,*
but I had already crossed that unfriendly steppe,
a day's drive, past bands of feral horses

and a few wooden shacks selling fruit brandy.
Brutal flashes of Miklós Jancsó's *Round-Up*
troubled me. I longed for Budapest, a human sprawl
someone might hope to hide in, even from Eichmann.

St Petersburg

Tsvetaeva gave Moscow to Mandelstam.
She led him as a stranger
to the Chapel of Inadvertent Joy,
over the Seven Hills, into churches,
through cemeteries – until he fled from her
as if she were a mist-wreathed nun,
back to his Parisian Petrograd, the city Peter
invented and Pushkin longed for –
to Nevsky Prospect, streetlights and an elegant
embankment. Nevertheless,
jagged images push up through his lines.
How else could he write,
in such an artificial city? growled a Moscow friend.
Think of Gogol. Or Dostoevsky!

Borscht in Odessa

Do you remember the September warmth,
perfumed with acacia when we first arrived?
And that street trader selling a greenish lizard,
with only a string securing its fierce mouth?
You put it on your arm for a photograph.

We were looking for traces of my grandfather
who lived in this city long ago.
Although the synagogues he would have known had burned
and Jews who stayed behind were likely dead,
strangely, we found others had returned:

doctors and poets, TV journalists, Chabad
and secular, some from the West
some from a childhood in Uzbekistan.
All remembered exile or evacuation,
and spoke, with a similar nostalgia,

of a city cosmopolitan as New York,
and Deribasovskaya, where
street cafés still serve salt herring and beer.
We listened to the talk
in the courtyard of Londonskaya hotel,

– once KGB headquarters – near the Steps. For days
we explored the graceful city centre,
taking a cab to Babel's Moldovanka.
Sadly, the archives did not record my grandfather –
and those with the same name weren't relatives.

In Odessa, they make the best borscht.
So I am preparing this soup tonight,
for you, dear son – gallant, Belmondo-lined –
because you travelled at my side
and met our failures with good-natured laughter.

A Dream of Prague

i.m. Miroslav Holub

Prague is a city of dreams without sleep:
Franz Kafka looking
at a whore near Zeltnerstrasse,
a lady in white silk
in the Kinsky Palace, shadows
on the Karlsbrücke,
ancient street lamps, wooden apostles
like sinister toys,
circling the astronomical clock.

Yet where else shall I think of you now
but in this city? Perhaps
when Havel was in the Castle behind
red and blue toy soldiers;
or in sunshine, with loud blackbirds on the hill
below the Summer Palace.
Mozart first heard his *Don Giovanni* cheered
in this golden Opera House,
and here it was we met you, looking relaxed,

not as in London or Cambridge, where
your eyes were always
hooded and cautious, a dapper-suited irony
beneath your courteous
reluctance to meet émigré friends,
your chance to travel
linked to nude mice and scientific papers
– not that wild carnival
of poetry: paradox and pepper.

In Prague, then, with casual euphoria,
– President now of the very
Writers' Union which once banned your poetry –
you led us to applaud
Jirí Menzel, the impudent director of
Closely Observed Trains,
wearing canvas sneakers in the Hotel Adria.
We ate in an Art Deco café,
green marble and mosaic restored.

Your enemies now were, chiefly, alternative medicine,
astrology and other superstitions,
and your face was alight with inspired mockery.
We shared in the amusement.
So why did we return home edgy and sad?
Three weeks later,
a Czech friend rang to tell us you were dead,
your witty spirit
sailing off into the starry darkness
over the Belvedere.

Tbilisi

Skewered lamb with almonds, champagne and Lermontov.
Poets loved Tbilisi in Soviet days. They flew south
from Moscow snows on rattling Aeroflot
over the peaks and chasms of the Caucasus,
to find sunshine, flowering chestnuts and acacia,
women with coppery hair and bare throats,
and men who looked like Italians, in loose shirts,
instead of ear-muffed Muscovites in winter coats.

In 1978, five British writers, released
from bugged hotels and grumpy minders *gardinage*
relished the street mix of faces and races.
We saw wooden houses, niched into a cliff,
with people eating breakfast on verandas
over a gorge with the yellow Kura below us –
a false step on a drunken afternoon would
test the healing waters of the Caucasus.

I remember the feasting, the Tamada, the toasts,
the licence given to Georgians as useful rogues
even in Moscow, where their market offered
slabs of beef, fresh fruit and green vegetables
illicitly driven north in *kholkhoz* lorries.
Last night, I watched on television as Russian tanks
were bullying old women in Georgian villages.
Times change, but it's rash to gamble on assistance.

Rush Cutter Bay, Sydney

Below us, the sea poured into the city,
silver and shimmering. We lay
together: hot, exhausted, happy.
Doesn't it often happen this way,
just before some unforeseen disaster
cuts you open with a casual
flick – like a knife stuck in an Asian fruit –
that the world feels particularly gentle?

The yachts danced below us
on shiny waters, there were
orange reflections in the windows.
How could I guess
the pain waiting on the next page for me?
The blank of betrayal which would
rapidly scoop out my life and release
the blood flow of poetry.

37

A Weekend in Berlin, 2008

for Martin

Has it disappeared, the world of George Grosz ?
  These days, no monocles leer
in the restaurants along the Ku'damm.
  Sensible burghers drink North German beer.

Almost, the city has become a museum
  which wears its history
– Reichstag, Checkpoint Charlie, Brandenberg Gate –
  with a gentle irony;

more affable than Soho, less raffish
  than Hamburg. We are tourists here,
eager to visit Liebeskind's new building.
  There is nothing to fear.

Only at the Hotel Adler, when
  a flunkey shakes his head
do I have a shiver of unease as if
  encountering the dead.

Kettle's Yard, Cambridge

It was happiness they painted, Renoir and Monet:
the delicate landscape of Chatou,
a boy running through a golden field of grass,
with dabs of red poppies, and flurried blue.

Kettle's Yard is sober in my memory:
quiet space and light on bare wood,
stone we could touch, the bronze Brancusi fish:
and contentment, much needed in a cold city.

A Night in Lisbon

for Ruth Fainlight

City of yellow trams and narrow streets, where
the women have eyes of darkness,
and in the Alfama washed clothes hang
over iron balconies.
Brothels and guitars hold the spirit of *fado*.

Last night, we listened to Mariza's voice.
She sang of female power and poverty,
her ashen, cropped hair and African face
an image taken out of Paula Rego:
strangeness − transmuted into beauty.

I remembered a night in Lisbon long ago,
in the palace of Fernando Mascarenhas,
the Marquis of Frontera and Alorna:
the ceilings were Renaissance frescoes,
his garden filled with classic *azulejos*.

A woman poet of genius was his ancestor.
Ruth and I were given single
beds in the dead poet's room as an honour
− and Ruth wanted to see her ghost.
Strangeness pleases her, curiosity

is her passion. Her wiry spirit, under
that forehead curve into
grizzled hair, is fired chiefly by a wish to know −
defiantly indifferent to status −
which makes for an integrity harsh as *fado*.

Three Fado Songs

from the Portuguese of Jose Carlos Ary dos Santos

Rose of Night

As I walk the streets at night time
my sadness is like basalt.
There's no pavement to protect me:
black rose of Portugal!

Silence makes a home inside me
within my own unhappy chest.
Night, you have undressed yourself
to give me tenderness.

I recognise my own pain now
in some abandoned dog, or
any lonely woman –
or an upturned rubbish bin.

On my shoulders I must carry
your street corners and balconies.
The bed on which I lie down
is made of cobblestones.

Light blue in the daylight,
dark blue in the night time.
When Lisbon holds no happiness
each star is like a blow.

Listen to a cat whine!
Somewhere a door screams.
A frigate on the Tagus
looks altogether dead,

I am dying piece by piece
for you, tormenting city!
I was born here and grew up
with your wind as my friend.

That's the reason I say: Lisbon,
every street is a throbbing vein,
and along each one a song runs
in my enormous voice.

The Tiles of Lisbon

Against a wall, or on a bench
these tiles mark all our yearning
in blue and white ceramic:
*azulejo*s of Lisbon!

They are pieces of my own life,
which has been glazed with sadness.
Let me say goodbye to each of them
with tears in my eyes.

On one a little girl, the next
a shepherd with his barking dog…
How every little frame becomes
a single poignant moment
in the picture book of love…

Poor faded tiles, you've seen
so many people crying!
How tired you must be
of those who pass you by!

Some of them reject you, or even
try to damage you
but I promise – you will never be
torn out of my heart.

Look! on the surface of each tile:
a carnation, or little bird,
a rocking horse, a pierced heart,
a holly bush. Their colour
is always moonlight blue –

the colour of the river Tagus.
There is an old boat on the shore –
I no longer see the distance –
and it fills Lisbon with childhood,
it fills Lisbon with the sea!

Alfama

When night falls over Lisbon
then the whole of the Alfama
becomes a ship without sails, or
a house without windows,
where people sit and grow cold.

And from some wretched garret
stolen from Alfama's misery,
locked inside four walls of water
– four stony walls of sobbing,
four walls of long disquiet –

at night a song will soar out
which lights up the whole city!
But Alfama, disenchanted,
still smells of melancholy.
It does not smell of *fado*

but of solitary people
sitting in a wounded silence
that tastes of bread and sadness.
Alfama does not smell of *fado* –
but it has no other song.

Arson in Hanià, Crete

for Nikos

Last August , in the windy hills where Cretans
      once gathered in monstrous caves
to fight the Germans, we were high above Hanià,
      by a blue pool. I was reading
Evelyn Waugh's *Sword of Honour*, learning
      how inept English manoeuvres lost the island
while the Resistance of the locals was triumphant.

We listened to immense cicadas, swam,
      and looked below at the Venetian harbour.
Then, one night, under a thin sliver of moon,
      we drove down a dusty track to Hanià
to buy presents of abalone or leather,
      and to meet Nikos Stavroulakis,
friend of a friend, who had spent ten years

obsessively restoring an old synagogue.
      He is from a family of *donmeh*
– that is, more Muslim than Jew, followers
      of Shabbatai Zevi – Nikos
survived the war in Turkey with his father.
      He is waiting for us peacefully
in a courtyard of gnarled trees: an erudite

eccentric, loving Byzantine art, West
      Cretan cookery, and his library
of ancient books and lost Sephardic melodies.
      The synagogue itself – an oddity –
the Jews in Crete were long ago deported
      and now only tourists visit,
directed by their guide books more than piety.

This winter, three louts climbed over his wall
    and lit a cushion soaked in paraffin.
Carpets were stained with soot, and paintwork smoked.
    For all the clatter in the streets,
few ran to douse the flames. Police were slow.
    Cretans are sullen, since
Greece became sick man of the Eurozone.

Two weeks later, perhaps incensed by scaffolding
    and signs of repair, the thugs returned –
and this time all the stacks of books were burned.
    They were two Brits, in Crete as waiters,
perhaps suborned, but certainly arrested,
    their motives dubious. I am told
Cretans resent American money and foreign builders.

Loss

Strange to find on this late slope of our lives,
two women ageing, and in my case alone,
who have passed through passions, illness,
disappointments, laughing off humiliations
now acknowledging we have drifted apart,

back into our own worlds, mine still Cambridge
or North London Jewish, yours the sharper
literati of Notting Hill. Visiting your cottage –
thirty-four years ago – I saw dogs in tree stumps
and listened to a song of family ghosts,

and since then we've shared lunch tables,
birthday flowers, dinner parties, telephone
secrets, most kept faithfully. Last time
we met we both had little to say.
Perhaps I bored you. When I came away,

I felt awkward and unhappy: there was no
quarrel, just s*omething that I failed to understand*,
your letter said. It's sad. I loved you once,
and would have called you at the Gates of Hell.
How do you revive a failing spell?

Christmas Day in Willesden Green

for my autistic grandchild

At fourteen, his eyes are dark as wood resin,
his hair red-gold; he is an elf-child
with delicate lips, and pale, unblemished skin.
The scented candles and the roasted goose
with apples in its throat don't interest him.
He flicks a dangled string and sets it loose

snatches a cracker biscuit, shaking off
the smoked fish, and then smiles suddenly
as if amused by some mischievous thought
growing out of a landscape I can't reach,
the unknown pathways lying under speech.
On these cold Christmas windows, heavy rain

begins, like the crackle of crumpled cellophane,
or an untuned radio; while Johnny remains soundless,
like a small bird gathering twigs and loam,
completely absorbed in his own business:
gold wrapping paper and coloured ribbons
are the treasures he brings to his sofa home.

It is the first year in seven the whole family
has eaten with him; we have feared his wild
behaviour and forgotten his misfortune,
as if that pain belonged to other people. Now he is mild,
we relax in noise and wine. Is he bewildered
among so many strangers, or reconciled?

Stetl in Belorus

after R.B. Kitaj, 'Babel Riding with Budyonny'

A swirl of ochre – then a brighter yellow
fills in the woodcut lines of an alien figure;
another stubby man wears a red scarf:
Carnival colours. What's the story here?

This is the euphoria of Revolution:
Ukraine in flames, the air a grey smoke.
Ash beneath dark skies. From a horse's white rump,
the colours turn in a kaleidoscope.

But where is Babel? Such insolence
for a myopic Jew – to ride
alongside Kuban Cossacks into Chagall's
villages of dirt-floor shacks.

The Whites have already trashed the *stetl.*
Babel rides with the Red Cavalry,
shamed by their courage, though they loot and kill.
Bystander angel, he records the dying.

Kitaj has sketched a man with a bird's head,
against the scribbled map of a little town,
an image styled after a medieval
Haggadah, telling the story of Passover.

Secrets of a shared family tree:
the faithful passions of the trapped,
the cheating promises of liberty –
Kitaj, like Babel, draws the savagery.

Festival in Tampico

Gulf of Mexico, 2006

Think of Bogart in the sad café
at the opening of John Huston's
Treasure of the Sierra Madre.
The film pervades the city:
iron shutters, shabby people, hot wet air.

By the red light district, repair
shops for sewing machines
and vacuum cleaners; not much trade.
In Plaza de la Libertad,
old men shine shoes among the pigeons.

We have arrived on the Day of the Dead,
hence these gaudy homemade dolls.
At dinner I refuse mescal, disliking *moriscos*,
and wondering, who is the invisible
patron of this Festival, who pays us

in used twenty dollar bills ? We have to be
fingerprinted before collecting.
Even stranger: in this depleted port of oil refineries
a Brazilian writer of detective stories
manages to convince me I'm still sexy.

Isaiah Berlin in Rome

At table with the guest of honour
on the Ambassador's terrace:
the heat is African. Tapers have been lit
to dispel mosquitoes.
We are eating flowers.

The deep lines on his face are humorous.
Dare I ask him, *What*
happened that night in Leningrad,
when Akhmatova
fell in love with you?

No.   He is deep in the torrent
of another story: his own terror
under Wittgenstein's questioning –
as every truthful answer,
exposes his poor claim to philosophy.

He acts it out and we are mesmerised.
The moon is full. White blossom leaks
perfume into the air. Virginia Woolf once
described him with unkind surprise:
a swarthy Portuguese Jew – until he speaks.

A Garden in North Germany

Moonlight, with snow falling tenderly
    over bare trees and conifers,
nestling in bushes: the whiteness
    of the garden enters me,

bloodless, vampiric, as if I were visiting
    my parents as a young wife,
to be pampered and safe, while the soul
    of my true rackety life

were being leeched out of me.
    Everyone is so kind
I have no strength to walk
    in the burning cold outside.

Dizzy in Westminster

Glossy black ringlets, blistering waistcoats, silver buckled shoes.
Where did you get the nerve for such flamboyance?
Not from your bookish father, skull-capped and scholarly,
whose anger with his Synagogue released you
into the gentile world, a baptised Jew.

Always in debt, and eager for renown, only
literary fame and a witty tongue gave you
entry to river parties and heady dinners
where politicians ate swans stuffed with truffles,
and married women readily became your tutors.

How did you bewitch those stolid gentlemen
of the shires to choose you for a leader?
Baptism did not make you less a Jew,
cartoonists mocked your aquiline profile
and drooping lip. But Parliament was your theatre.

Across the Dispatch Box, Gladstone
disliked your eloquence and found you
slippery, your talent opportunist –
while you thought him a prig. Let us
confess your policy imperialist,

your cleverest foreign deals somehow
congruent with your own extravagance.
Yet courage trumps all and demands tribute.
You flattered, entertained, but never cringed.
And that, dear Earl of Beaconsfield, I salute.

Prizes

A cold wind. A clear sky. Wet branches
sizzle this morning in the sunlight.
Take no notice of the man behind the curtain.
You can always get back to Kansas. If you know
where home is, you don't have a problem.
Look at this gifted man, unshaven, smiling.

He grounds himself in the rich soil
of Irish poetry, and puts away his angry fear
of being forgotten, alongside the hope
of prizes: knowing those blobs of glory,
to be trinkets in the jewellery shop window
which is the human imagination of eternity.

Butterflies Lost

Childhood I remember as hot summer,
with butterflies on bushes of blue Syringa,
their chocolate brown wings and orange bands,
trembling in the dizzy sweet of nectar.
I tried to catch one as a child of nine,
to stroke the velvet throbbing in my hands,
as if it were a delicate tabby cat
but the fluttering died. In whose hands did they fall,
those later generations of Red Admirals?
What human convenience brought them down?
There are none in my London garden now –
only a few Cabbage Whites, with edges
yellow as fading news pages –
though I have planted bushes of blue flowers.

Sweet Corn

for Rachel

One day, as a young girl, will you remember
this necklace with beads of pale amber
brought home from a market stall in Odessa?
At five you called them *Sweet corn*:
an innocent error making a metaphor.
I wonder if you will bring together
other disparate things as you grow older
or whether as a clever
young woman you will forget
the moment you almost became a poet?

Long Life

Late summer. Sunshine. The eucalyptus tree.
It is a fortune beyond any deserving
to be still *here*, with no more than everyday worries,
placidly arranging lines of poetry.

I consider a stick of cinnamon
bound in raffia, finches
in the grass, and a stubby bush
which this year mothered a lemon.

These days I speak less of death
than this miracle of survival. I am
no longer lonely, not yet frail, and
after surgery, recognise each breath

as a favour. My generation may not be
nimble but, forgive us,
we'd like to hold on, stubbornly
content − even while ageing.